LIGHTW🔆RKERS

www.lightworkersllc.com

LIGHTWORKERS

188 Jefferson Street, Suite 324

Newark, NJ 07105

ISBN: 0-578-40309-9
ISBN-13: 978-0-578-40309-0
Library of Congress Control Number (LCCN): 2018912456

Manufactured in the United States of America

Editor-in-Chief: Fatou Simone Seydi

Contributing Editor: Tyrone Webb Jr.

Cover design by Tamara Williams

i

don't

know how

i got here

but here

i am

SHARON ELISE

DEDICATION

Dear Savannah,

It's been said that younger generations are incapable of learning from older generations' mistakes; that we all go through the same phases of life, yet somehow believe our experiences are unique to the times we are living. This is my attempt of shattering that notion. You can learn from what I've been through instead of making the same mistakes. There will be things you will need to learn on your own and I pray that I will give you the space to learn, flourish, and grow through your life experiences. Know that you are whole, though the world may make you feel like you are not good enough. Stand firm in the truth that you are enough, just as you are right now. I love you forever.   This   is   for   you.

CONTENTS

Acknowledgments   i

Manifesto of Truth   iii

He's Called Me Out   vii

Hello World   1

Big Battle   10

Finding Myself   21

Nothing Changes Without Changes   34

Metamorphosis   50

O' Ye of Little Faith   61

Forgiveness   71

Love for One's Self   81

Facing Fear   91

Believe in Yourself   100

Distractions   110

Dream, Plan, Act   120

Epilogue

Afterword

ACKNOWLEDGEMENTS

All the glory, honor and praise goes to GOD, the head of my life, the creator of all things, the Universal Higher Power that cannot be defined. I am in awe of Your work.

I give thanks to my parents, Ursula Hudson and Calvin Swan, Jr., for their spirits joining together in the creation of my being. I am forever grateful for your sacrifice, service, and love.

To my husband and life partner, Vincent, thank you for joining me on this journey and providing a reflection of growth and love. You came into my life at just the right time. I look forward to growing in love with you.

To Savannah, my moon, my light in the midst of darkness, thank you for choosing me as your mother and spirit guide. Thank you for loving me unconditionally. I am a better person because of you. I love you and aspire to be as loving, kind, and joyful as you. Never let anyone dim your light baby girl. It shines bright!

To Solomon, my sun, my light after the storm, thank you for choosing me as your mother and spirit guide. Though at the time of this publishing, you are not yet born into the physical world, your presence and energy has been felt already. I look forward to witnessing all that you'll become and the light that you'll bring to the world. You are loved by many.

To Jihad, my brother and "bishop", thank you for your guidance, wisdom, and friendship. Over the years, we've journeyed through a lot of terrains together, navigating whatever storms life has thrown our way. Knowing that as long as we had each other, we'd survive anything. Thank you for choosing me as your sister. It's been the highest honor and greatest calling in my life.

To all of my family and friends, those who are named and those who names are unknown, my ancestors, kin, and descendants. Thank you for your light, love, and life. I appreciate and love you all dearly. I give thanks for each of you. Gbogbo ifẹ mi! *All my love.*

MANIFESTO OF TRUTH

From a very early age, I'd dreamt of being a writer. Many times sitting down to write this book I experienced much resistance. I didn't believe my story was valuable and was afraid of sharing intimate details of my life in a vulnerable way. I was scared of being judged and experienced a great deal of guilt and shame. Writing this book took me to some dark spaces that I'd much rather suppress and forget ever existed. The past does not go away, and though we shouldn't dwell on it, the past can be beneficial to revisit with intention to stimulate growth, transformation, and healing. I wouldn't have been able to navigate through the things I've been through had I not been willing to take an honest look at the past. You cannot know where you're heading without knowing where you've been.

This book is an expression of the knowledge and lessons I've learned thus far. I share them in hopes that it will change your perspective of life and awaken you to the truth of your being. You do not have to like, understand, or even agree with anything that I share. All I ask is that you are open to receiving it.

I've had my fair share of hard times and tragedy, but over time I've learned to accept suffering and I've learned to navigate through it. Life has not always been good to me, but I've survived. I strive daily to be better than I was the day before. I own my imperfections. I will never claim to be more than I am. This is the truth of my being. This is who I am. I am not an expert nor do I claim to be. I am aware and acknowledge that I do not have all the answers and am still learning life's lessons.

Life is intended to be experienced in fullness. While there may be things that you regret and/or wish you could change about your life, everything that has occurred, good-or-bad has a divine purpose. Your life has shaped you into the person you are. If anything were different, you would not be who you are today. Be thankful for the lessons, they've propelled you to the next level of your life.

The truth is you already know everything you need to know. Perhaps you've forgotten or refuse to harness your innate power. It is the inability to tap into your authentic power that creates chaos, distraction, and suffering in your life. You may expect to breeze through life uninflected by struggle when you are, in fact creating those very experiences that are causing you dis-ease. You do not have to remain inflicted by your discomfort. You can learn to live with suffering and use it as a catalyst to move forward.

Life is not always easy, and if anyone says that it is, run far away. This person has chosen to settle, and my guess is that if you are reading this book you do not settle. You push forward striving to be better than you were yesterday. I invite you to join me on this journey of growth, healing, and elevation through the stories, revelations, and insights I share.

It is my prayer that this book is as much a blessing to you reading it, as it has been for me writing it. Learning to face my fears has and continues to remind me to open myself to receiving all that life has to offer. Ultimately I grew into my best Self because of it. I pray the same for you.

This is the journey and the lessons I've learned along the way.

HE'S CALLED ME OUT

He's called me out.

Out of my shell.

Slowly peeking out, I see the light.

Glowing from his inner being.

He is God and he's introducing me to a world I never

knew.

I'm in heaven.

Where the sun is always shining and the sky is truly

blue.

I hear music. I see stars.

I feel the vibrations of the Earth.

He is I and I am He.

We are One.

This is love.

He's called me out.

Out to face my fears.

To be bold. To be brave. To be fearless.

He's walked beside me into the lion's den.

Holding my hand and never letting go.

He will never leave my side.

He's a treasure.

A precious jewel.

I will never let go.

We are One.

This is love.

He's called me out.

Out to live in my truth.

The Truth.

In his presence, I grow taller with the passing of each
day.

I am 10 feet tall.

He's exposed me to new depths and heights.

Places that I believed were out of my reach.

He's a reflection of me.

He's a King. My King.

And I, His Queen.

We are One.

And this is L O V E.

HELLO WORLD

"To live is to suffer, to survive is to find
some meaning in the suffering."
~Friedrich Nietzsche~

On June 12, 1987, at exactly 9:31 a.m., I was born into the world. I imagine kicking and screaming, wondering why I'd chosen to experience life yet again. At a very young age I could sense there was something different about me. I was always asking questions and wondering about the purpose of my life. I believe we are all born with innocence and truth of our connection to a Higher Power, but we lose sight of this somewhere in our journey - we experience some sort of suffering that separates us from God. For me, it was the death of my father.

At the age of seven, on a hot, spring day, I returned home from school, to play outside with my friends before dinner. When I got off the van, I noticed there was something different about my house as I walked towards the front porch. The door was wide open, which it never was, as we always kept the doors locked. As I walked into the living room I noticed my grandmother sitting on the sofa, she looked as though she had been crying. I asked her, "What is wrong?" She told me to go upstairs, my mother needed to talk to me. I immediately thought, "What did I do now?" Had I forgotten to do the dishes the night before? My mind raced as I thought of all the things I could have possibly done to be in trouble. My hopes of going outside were shattered.

When I reached the top of the stairs, I knocked on my mother's bedroom door, she was sitting on the edge of her bed crying. Something was definitely different in my house. Until that day I'd never seen my mother cry, not even at her grandmother's funeral; my grandmother always said she was the strong one. So what could it be that was bringing my mother to tears? She told me to sit down next to her. It was then that she told me my father had passed away and I wouldn't see him again. I did not know what she meant by passed away. She mouthed something about him always being in my heart but I could no longer hear her. I rushed out of her room and into the bathroom. I closed and locked the door and didn't come out until the banging on the door became unbearable. I'd been crying so hard until my eyes were red and puffy and my appetite was gone. I remember going to bed without dinner that night.

The next couple of weeks were hard to get through. I missed a few days of school, which the school administrators understood, considering my father's death was on the news and in newspapers. The night before my father's memorial service, my mom and stepmother took my brother and I to my grandparents' house to discuss the preparations for my father's service with my family members. I can recall a lot of arguing between the adults. I sheltered my brother from the chaos by showing him pictures of our dad and vowing to always protect him. We sat on my grandmother's couch looking through pictures, as tears rolled down my face. I hugged my brother tightly. I did not understand why this was happening to us. "Aren't children supposed to grow up with both parents?" I pondered on this over and over.

Many people were in attendance at the memorial service - some I knew and others I did not. My father was cremated which I did not have a clear understanding of at the time. All I knew was in the marble "dish" at the front of the room were the ashes of the only man I'd ever loved, my daddy, my superhero, and best friend. And now he was gone. I wasn't ready for his death and I couldn't imagine living life without him.

Was he truly in my heart as my mom said? What did that mean? Why couldn't I see him? Talk to him? Hug him? These were all questions that I wanted to ask but never did. I am not sure I would have received clear answers anyway. All I knew was my dad was gone and I would never see him again.

My mother and I never talked about my father's death. She never asked how his death affected me or discussed him in great detail after his death. I do recall her asking me occasionally if I'd missed him. I can imagine that my mother struggled with my father's death, yet neither of us ever discussed it. We never talked about her feelings or mine for that matter.

While I wasn't privy to her emotions, I do know that the loss of my father had a major toll on my mother financially. In the wake of his tragic death, she went from being in a co-parenting relationship to being a single mother. As far back as I can remember my mother has always had more than one job. The numerous jobs created distance between us; I grew to resent her because I couldn't understand why was she always at work, unable to spend more time with me, to do things like help with my homework as she used to.

I grew up in a Baptist church, every Sunday until 4th grade, the year following my father's death, I was required to be in a pew at church. It was this religious foundation that contributed to my healing. There were several occasions that I sat in my room, kneeling, praying to God for answers. The harder I cried, the harder I prayed. I could feel the protection and warmth of God's love over my life. I just didn't quite understand and refused to accept "everything in life has a purpose" as an answer to my questions. I wanted tangible results, I wanted my father back, but I realized that was never going to happen. The only way I could make it through life was to keep moving forward. And so I did.

Lesson: *All suffering leads to healing.*

In life, we are all born into suffering. It is our suffering that makes us human. Without it, we'd be stagnant, dead, lifeless; yet life is a cycle of evolution and elevation. As we grow through life, we will experience many cycles of suffering that call for a response. Although there may be times that it appears easier to wallow in sorrow, wishing for things to be different, everything has a divine purpose. The passing of a loved one, financial hardships, or a romantic heartbreak may have been a part of your suffering, however, you survived. Every good or bad thing that has ever happened to you was for a purpose. Your purpose is rooted in your spirit, the part of you that knows innately who you truly are.

We are all born with special gifts, unique talents to add meaning and value to the world. As we journey through life we lose conscious awareness of our connection to our purpose. Our suffering becomes debilitating and we lose sight of the journey to finding purpose. We become prisoners of the mind, held captive by the fear of our suffering.

We then blame external factors for our inability to move forward without accepting responsibility for our lives. Refusing to see ourselves for the divine beings that we are, it becomes easier to accept that you have no control over your life because you are freed of responsibility. Once we remember that we are the authority over our lives, no one – not parents, partners, government, society, friends, or circumstance – can define or become the creator of our lives.

Suffering is part of life however, there are many ways out. In the chapters that follow are the blueprint for how I found my way out of suffering. I learned to see my way through it and found light on the other side. This is not my plan, it's God's. I simply accepted it, I live it, and I walk in my truth. From a young age to present day, I've learned to accept the fact that every seemingly difficult experience in my life yields fruits of valuable lessons. Ultimately, I am a stronger, better person because of the traumatic and painful events I experienced. What was once debilitating and defeating became a source of strength and growth to continue along the journey.

BIG BATTLE

"Turn your wounds into wisdom."
~Oprah Winfrey~

The next few years were difficult to get through. In addition to my father's death at the end of fourth-grade, I also transitioned to a new school for fifth grade. Like most middle schoolers, I spent most of fifth and sixth grade hanging out with the wrong people. Their parents were cool and allowed them to spend nights out; opposed to the strict rules that I had to follow that didn't allow me to sleepover any of my friends' houses. Always an "A" student, my grades started to slip by the end of the year.

Until I was a "B-C" student, rebelling against my mother and smoking almost every day. My friends and I would sneak cigarettes from our mothers' purses to smoke in the park after school. We were mimicking the behaviors of our mothers and believed the cigarettes somehow relieved our stress. This pattern continued as I progressed through school and my behavior spiraled out of control.

I was numb. Though I had a relationship with Him, I was angry with God. I wanted my father back. Every year without him was hard. I was desperate for my mother's attention and yearning for my father's love. Though I knew life wouldn't be perfect, I constantly imagined how different my life would be if my father was alive.

I was disconnected from God but wasn't ready to heal old wounds. I continued walking blindly through the world, becoming a leech, sucking the life out of everyone around me. I was walking around beaten up and bruised, expecting the people in my life to show up wholly for me, though I didn't have the tools to show up wholly for myself. I was sad, lonely, and depressed. When you are not whole in yourself you cannot give to anyone.

The year following my father's death, I rebelled against my mother, refusing to do my chores, staying out past curfew, and skipping school to hang out with friends. While my mother was working, I was left under the supervision of my grandmother, which lacked attention, emotionality, and connection, all things I needed during this traumatic time of grief and loss.

My lack of respect for my mother increased as I continued to rebel, doing what I wanted to do. She started picking me up from school to ensure I made it home every day. I'd long since started hanging out late after school, coming in after dark. It didn't work. Once my mother returned to work, I'd be under the supervision of my grandmother. I started sneaking out after she'd fall asleep on the sofa watching soap operas.

I was bullied most of sixth grade year, only standing up for myself after being pressured by my mother and cousin to "just fight." I fought and I won, but I'm not really sure what. There was no prize waiting for me, other than a boosted ego, I didn't gain much of anything. I spent the remainder of the year in the "Calm Room' as punishment for getting into a physical altercation on school property.

I didn't quite understand why fighting was a skill I was just supposed to know how to do. My mother would be angry with me for coming home crying almost every day from the torment of girls trying to force me to fight. I didn't want to and wasn't really confident I knew how. All I wanted to do was go to school to learn. Why did I have to learn how to defend myself in a place that was designed to stimulate my mind? Instead, it endangered it.

After fighting my bully, I ended up being removed from the place I wanted to be most: the classroom. This didn't make any sense. It was at this point school started to seem pointless. I recognized then that it wasn't a place to learn, but a place to be liked and accepted. I yearned to fit in.

I began seventh grade at yet another new school where I didn't know anyone. My mother thought I'd be better suited at a private school where the focus was more on education and less on socialization. The thing is socialization is all school seemed to be good for. Outside of attending our classes, the focus was mainly on who liked or didn't like who. Even though I tried to stay under the radar, I was naturally a kid who wanted to be everyone's friend. I didn't like that there were cliques. I would write about this in my diary a lot. I showed up with a calm demeanor, but not knowing the structure that existed in social groups, I landed in the center of drama anyway.

Due to unresolved pain, I continued to attract more drama. Two weeks before eighth-grade graduation I ended up getting into a fight and getting suspended. The principal questioned whether I should graduate. I couldn't believe this was happening. I felt ashamed. In the end, I did graduate and looked forward to beginning high school with a fresh start.

I began the first day of high school at Saint Vincent Academy, an all- girls Catholic school, with a Winnie-the-Pooh backpack filled with notebooks, art supplies, and writing utensils. I was eager for this new start, yet I managed to get kicked out of three classes during the first week of school: I hadn't yet learned to hold my tongue and have always been one to speak my mind. My mother would always tell me "think before you speak", but back then I really didn't understand why.

While my overall high school experience was an enjoyable one, it's not one that I'd ever want to repeat. I wished so much to not have to go to school. My grades were average because I did the bare minimum to pass. Looking back, it was one of the most depressing times of my life, but mostly because I hadn't yet found myself. I spent most of those years searching for something, not really sure of what.

I'd long since stopped attending church after being scolded by one of the elders for wearing a summer dress during Revival week fifth grade year. It was a huge deal in my house about me not going. My grandmother and cousins went every Sunday and I was expected to attend as well. I told my mother why I didn't want to go and she supported my decision.

During my freshman year, I started going to church with anyone who would invite me, but never felt compelled to return after my first visit. It was a space I no longer felt welcome. I was searching for God in the place where I was supposed to feel Him most, but all I could feel was isolation and rejection. I carried around a ton of emotions from my father's death, coupled with teenage hormones, let's just say those weren't my finest years.

It didn't help that my mother and I weren't as close as we used to be. She was still working multiple jobs to cover my school's tuition. The frequency with which we saw each other was like we were ship's passing in the night. I'd tried to connect with God through the Bible, but during that time, I didn't fully understand what I was reading. It must have had some impact. In one diary entry during my sophomore year, I wrote, "Jesus is the key to unlock ALL doors." If only I was putting this faith into action. Instead of drawing closer to God, naturally I sought out comfort from people, places, and things.

I wasn't ready to return to God, even though my soul was yearning for it. Sometimes I would sit on the floor in my room and just cry until my stomach hurt. I was angry with God and as a result I was angry with the world. I didn't have any regard for anyone. I lashed out at people without thinking about my actions. I was being hurtful, simply because I was hurting.

During that time in my life, my spirit was searching for something, but my ego was broken. I walked around with so much anger and hurt, I couldn't recognize that I was broken. My spirit submitted and my ego carried the suffering of my father's death for over seventeen years. I wore it as a badge of honor all those years, refusing to let go of the suffering. It became a battle between my ego and spirit, fighting for balance and control.

In order to advance along my journey, I had to be willing to accept all of me. I learned to acknowledge and accept the space of fear, doubt, conceit, dishonesty, and manipulation. I had to embrace the parts of myself that were "not so favorable" so that I could embrace the totality of my being. I had to be willing to go through the chaos in order to find myself.

Lesson: The hurt you give, is the hurt you receive.

The behavior of the ego is neither negative nor positive, it just is. Though we are born into suffering, it does not have to cause any further pain. It's not the suffering that causes our pain, it's our ego - our attachment to the story the mind creates about the pain we are experiencing. The ego is an aspect of your being and manifests itself through your thoughts, feelings, and behaviors. It is not a thing per se, but a mental state of being. It is manipulative, deceiving, and untrustworthy. The ego feels threatened and attacked when it does not or cannot have its' way. It fights to be seen, heard, and feared. The ego believes that it is always right.

Ego is just one aspect of who we are. Our human existence is made up of both ego and spirit. The true nature of our being is a balance between the two. To reach the space where ego and spirit co-exist, you have to first acknowledge the presence of ego. Denying the existence of ego will only advance detrimental behavior and stagnate growth.

The ego is the part of yourself that likes to believe that you are always right, has all the answers, and knows what is best for you and those around you. The ego believes that it is the boss. It likes to control your daily functioning, thinking, and behaviors. Your spirit is calmer in nature, refuses to fight the battle and is not easily angered. Your spirit recognizes that total peace cannot be reached without the compliance of ego, but chooses to disengage from the battle to avoid further conflict. Ego wants to reign over your life without having the proper tools, while spirit not only has the tools, but also has your highest intention in mind.

You will continue to experience this struggle between ego and spirit throughout your lifetime. With persistency and patience, you must learn to work to create balance and stability between the two. Otherwise, your life will be controlled by instabilities and inconsistencies of your mind. One cannot exist without the other. Both makeup aspects of who you truly are and once you are capable of maintaining both, a world of peace and happiness will be revealed to you.

FINDING MYSELF

"Knowing yourself is the beginning of all wisdom."

~Artistotle~

If you'd asked me during college if I knew who I was, I would have eagerly replied, "absolutely." When in fact, I was just at the beginning of the discovery. Even now, I am learning, growing, and enjoying the process of getting to know myself. It's a life long road. I will always have blind spots, parts of myself that I am unaware of that are in need of more love and healing. I call them areas of growth, places God has left as a reminder of my connection to a Higher Power.

As a young adult, I made a lot of excuses for my choices and behaviors. I thought I knew everything when really I was naïve and had much to learn. I was a difficult person to be around because I had no self-worth. I fought for attention and filled space with things to block the silence that comes with being alone. I was afraid to be with alone myself because I was lost and broken. Friends had broken up with me, some family had broken up with me; I had all but broken up with myself.

I felt so alone in the world, without anyone to talk to who I felt would understand me. I started to lose myself in the people around me. I'd latch on to anyone I felt could fulfill me in places I didn't even know were empty. I was navigating the world without any clear vision of where I was heading or what I was doing.

As a child growing up I was conditioned to seek outside validation for my behaviors. I learned whether my actions were favorable or displeasing to my mother based on her responses: a smile or clap communicated favorable behavior while a yell or punishment did not. As I grew older, I continued to seek outside validation from my mother, family members, and friends due to lack of awareness of my desire for validation, which continued to increase as I grew older and sought approval for things like fashion, relationships, and career choices.

The validation provided the confirmation I was looking for that I could not ultimately give to myself. I was allowing other people to direct my life, making choices based on their opinions, perceptions, and judgments, without ever considering my own. Although the people I sought counsel from provided good advice, how could I allow anyone else to decide what was best for me without knowing for myself? I had to build confidence in my decision-making and be willing to make mistakes in order to learn and grow in the process.

I can still recall the first time I treated myself to a solo movie date. I didn't make any announcement or ask anyone to join me. I just went. I saw Twilight Saga: New Moon. I'd finished the book series and was excited to see it on the Big Screen. I sat in a back row seat, next to two older women who were chaperoning their teenagers on a date but weren't allowed to sit near them. I enjoyed our conversation before the movie. I overcame fear of being alone and felt this sense of peace after leaving the theater. I had finally discovered the serenity of time spent alone.

It takes a great deal of strength to be alone with your thoughts and witness as they ebb and flow. As I started spending more time alone, I noticed my thoughts began to run wild. I couldn't control them and would ride the wave of uncertainty, confusion, and doubt. That was until I was able to gain control over my thoughts. This occurred only after I acknowledged my separation from the voice in my head.

As I became more focused on my healing the desire to be around other people slowly vanished, as I continued to spend more time alone. Lunch, movies, mall trips, I loved creating space to take myself on mini dates and enjoyed the solace. I started learning more about myself, what I liked, what I didn't like; I revisited past hurts, guilt, and failures. It was a painful process, but one I'm grateful for. It required a great deal of confidence, strength, and endurance. Throughout the process I had to make some hard decisions and was faced with many challenges; however, it brought me to peace. I started reading more, cut my hair, and even started writing again. I was able to get back to the essence of me. I chose to accept responsibility for my actions, instead I instead of making excuses for my choices. This was much different from previous experiences.

Defensiveness became a strong indicator of change. Anytime I became defensive about something, it served as an indicator of an area of growth. Becoming defensive does not resolve the problem it exposes it. I would only be defensive about things that I was not yet consciously aware of and was not ready to accept. If someone said I was selfish, I agreed because I knew that to be true about myself. A different response would be elicited when someone would say I was mean. I'd become defensive, combative, and readily engaged in heated arguments, as an attempt to protect my character, when in fact I was tarnishing it.

I didn't want to see myself as that person, when in fact, that's a part of who I was. I created excuses for my attitude, I justified my actions and refused to acknowledge that as an aspect of my personality. In moments like those, I refused to see myself from any vantage point other than my own. A stance like that is disastrous. It creates a one-dimensional view of life, which leads to stagnation, by refusing to accept the perception of others.

When you spend your entire life being told who to be, how to act, and what to say, you become reliant on other people's opinion of who you should be instead of relying on yourself. You should never grant anyone that much power over your life. It became clear to me that there was something for me to learn about myself. From then on, anytime someone said or did something that made me feel uncomfortable or defensive, I chose to use it as a learning moment. I didn't want to project my feelings on anyone without acknowledging their perspective. I had to be willing to listen to what was being said, in place of projecting my responses, attributing them to external factors outside of myself. Projection does not cause healing, even if it may temporarily serve as a release, it does, however, perpetuate an unconscious cycle of denial, guilt, and shame.

If balance is finding yourself, then totally rejecting another's perspective is a state of imbalance. I had to be open to seeing myself through the eyes' of others in order to grow in the areas I could not see for myself, but I had to learn to see myself first, to love myself, first. I had to find the balance between pride and humility. Owning who I am and accepting the good with the bad, but no longer making excuses. Needing an excuse for anything signals something is off balance that needs to be addressed, otherwise, I wouldn't continue in this pattern of conduct. I don't have to be defensive, argumentative or even respond when someone shares their perspective, whether I agree with it or not.

Although I made some choices along my journey that I wouldn't make now, I don't regret anything. Everything that has occurred paved the way for me to be here. Every step that I made whether good, bad, or indifferent, had a purpose. I could choose to live life in regret of the choices I've made, stuck in a repetitious cycle of guilt and shame or I could accept my journey, heal from it and move forward.

Lesson: Knowledge of self is of the highest order.

Most of us lack insight into who we are that often times we can't recognize when we are lost and disconnected from ourselves. In fact, many of us suppress parts of ourselves out of fear of rejection, shame, and guilt. We choose to turn a blind eye to the less desirable parts, taking on a version of ourselves that we believe embodies perfection. We put on masks, becoming someone that we are not just to be accepted in a society that says we aren't good enough.

To know who you are, you must begin to shed the masks that have been created by the people in your life - the people that have impacted your personality and shaped the person you believe yourself to be like your parents, family, partners, friends, etc. You've spent the majority of your life being told who to be, now it's time to discover who you are for yourself. In order to fully love yourself, you must first recognize and acknowledge the totality of your being. This means accepting the good with the bad.

Unfortunately, we are born into a world that sends contradictory messages about what it means to be you. Parents teach their children 'it's what's on the inside that counts' when society communicates it's the outside that really matters. Whole groups of people are rejected, ridiculed, and outcast for looking, talking, acting, and even loving differently. Quite frankly, it's hard to be your unique self in a world that refuses to accept individuality.

In order for the world to accept individuality, we each must display courage and pride for the totality of our being, accepting all of who we are. Instead we cast out the parts of ourselves that are displeasing, unfavorable, and unacceptable, choosing to accept boxes that have been created for us to fit in. We hide in closets, behind closed doors, and shedding endless amounts of tears, hoping to be accepted, loved, and appreciated for who we really are.

We can no longer choose to accept the good without the "bad." Our differences aren't intended to separate us, but shed light on the uniqueness of our being. We must free ourselves from the illusion of perfection and allow our flaws, vulnerabilities, and insecurities to shine bright. They are apart of who we are. We do not need to wear masks, pretending to be perfect because we all are perfectly imperfect. Be willing to take a good look in the mirror and see yourself for who you really are. Can you acknowledge and honor the parts of yourself that you love while also looking at your flaws and still be at peace with the person staring back at you?

There are an infinite amount of perspectives that exist in the world. Each individual has a unique viewpoint based on the experiences in their reality. To reject someone's perspective, totally, is refusing to acknowledge the multitude of perceptions that exist within this universe. Instead of using a limited perspective, looking at yourself through an alternative lens provides an opportunity to experience the fullness of yourself.

Everyone's perception is based on individual experiences. One can choose to truly listen to what is being said and aim for understanding without solely listening to respond. You don't have to agree with the other perspective, but it doesn't make it any less true for the person living that experience. Listening to what others have to say will increase your understanding of not only of yourself but also the world. Instead of making excuses, make adjustments, starting with whatever may be imbalanced.

Be open to the experience of discovery, both internally and externally. The process of self-discovery will lead you to making connections between the internal work and the external feedback you receive from the people in your life. We are the sum of the five people to whom we are the closest. If you do not like the behaviors and characteristics of someone you are connected to, begin with why? Deep reflection may reveal similar aspects within yourself. Life is not stable and there will always be room for growth. The challenge is to overcome the feelings of fear, associated with change, in order to address the disconnection between who you are and who you want to be. You cannot live in peace and harmony projecting a reality of perfection and wholeness where there's a need for transformation and healing. You have to be willing to be still and reflect on your areas of growth. Ultimately you'll find yourself waiting on the other side.

NOTHING CHANGES WITHOUT CHANGES

"Sometimes there's chaos in balance."

~Felicia Johnson~

It took me four years to figure out what I wanted to do with my life. After securing a job at a Fortune 500 company straight out of college, making more money than any twenty-one-year-old with no responsibilities probably should have at the time, I thought I was headed towards a life of financial gains and security. Yet after working for the company for five years, including a one-year internship during college, I was ready to quit. Even though there were many benefits including working from home, it was one of the most miserable times of my life. I wasn't doing what I loved and no amount of money could compensate for that. I decided to return to school to work towards a Master's degree in Psychology, with the dream of becoming a therapist.

At the time, everyone around me thought I was crazy to leave a secure job to return to school, especially when I was making "good money" and got to work from home. I didn't care about the luxury of at-home work or the decent salary. I knew there was no way I was going to make my dreams come true with only a bachelor's degree. At best I could obtain an entry-level position making half of what I was making at the Fortune 500 company and this was not the life I wanted.

After two stressful years of graduate school, working two jobs to make up for the salary pay cut, maintaining above a 3.5 GPA, and holding no less than 18 credits per semester, I graduated. I think it was midway through my Master's program that I realized I didn't want to be a therapist. I couldn't stop going to school though. I thought to myself, "Who drops out of graduate school!?" It didn't make sense. I couldn't justify it and continued the work to complete my program and graduate.

I applied to a few doctoral programs after a classmate shared that he'd applied to at least twelve. I thought, "If he could apply to that many, I can at least apply to one." In dealing with family stress and a bad break-up, I was ready for a change of scenery. I'd never left home before so the thought of being in a new city, was both exciting and nerve-wracking.

I applied to two doctorate programs and I was accepted to a program in New Hampshire, moved to Massachusetts and drove 2 1/2 hours to school every week. I refused to move to a place where there weren't many people that looked like me. It was a fear I wasn't ready to face at that time. For me, it wasn't about getting the education, it was about getting away. For the first time in my life, I would have the opportunity to be alone, in a new space without anyone or anything familiar.

The first night in my apartment, as I stood on the balcony on a late summer night, with a glass of wine, thanking God for the blessing, I cried not knowing what was to come. I questioned my decision and worried about my immediate future. I moved to Massachusetts with less than $3,000 in my bank account and with no job prospects. With what was in my savings, I had enough to survive for three months. I had faith that God would make a way.

Two months passed, nearly at the point of crawling back home with tales of failed dreams, facing eviction if I didn't find a job, I landed a position as an in-home therapist. I was grateful, but after a few months, I started to feel it wasn't a good fit. I was only paid for the times I was with clients and was spending more money getting to them than I was getting paid. I remembered to pray.

After just four months, and barely making ends meet, one day I had the thought to quit my job. I just couldn't take it any longer and felt the job wasn't worth the stress. I knew I could manage to survive a few months off my student loan refund until I secured another position. I also had a work-study through my doctoral program so I felt comfortable quitting my job. The day I started to work on my resignation letter I received a call for an interview at a local community college for an adjunct faculty position I'd applied for. I left the office immediately and went to the interview, confident that the position would be mine. I received the call the next day that I was hired and printed out the resignation letter and placed it in my supervisor's mailbox. I couldn't have been happier.

With a flexible schedule and secure income, I once again had more time to dive into self inquiry without stressing over getting bills paid. Forced again to face inner darkness, I had to uproot the wounds of my past in order to heal. I could no longer turn a blind eye to the things that had manifested in my life. I couldn't remain a victim of my past, I had to let it go. The good thing about studying Psychology is that it forced me to take an honest and informed look at myself.

So there I was, a 25-year old woman trying to figure her life out away from home and everything familiar. I was in the jungle, so to speak, and scared shitless. The first year away I spent a lot of time in solitude. My process could have easily been diagnosed as depression, but I was able to recognize the beauty in that space. Growing up in a house, where there was someone always home, this was the most time I'd spent alone since being a fetus in my mother's womb.

I was scared to be alone with my thoughts when they were unrelenting and chaotic. I had to get over the feelings of loneliness to get comfortable in my aloneness. I had to learn to be comfortable in quiet and stillness, something that was foreign and uncomfortable initially. This time alone provided the opportunity for me to get to know myself. Things that I wasn't able to recognize while I was in a constant state of familiarity, I found in solitude.

In solitude, I was able to recognize that I was a broken soul. This self-discovery provided the space for me to heal in order to be a better person, not for anyone other than myself. This was for me. It was a painful process with a lot of crying, but it prepared me for my breakthrough.

I remained in New England for two years, completing all academic requirements, with only a clinical internship and dissertation left to complete, I decided to return home to pursue a job opportunity to satisfy my internship requirements and to begin work on my dissertation. After months of interviews without any prospects of employment, I realized that securing full-time work wasn't going to be as easy as I'd initially thought.

I spent months unemployed. One month turned into ten, ten months turned into fourteen. I thought returning to school to gain knowledge and experience in the field would leave me with the ability to land a job working in an office, earning a decent salary, and paying off my student loan debt. Instead, I spent the next two years living at home with my mother, unemployed, and depressed. With the exception of a part-time job during the holiday season at a bookstore, I was otherwise professionally unemployed.

During that time, I would pray and ask for guidance and felt that I should take a leave of absence from school, but my pride wouldn't let me. I started asking family and friends if they thought I should quit. I wasted a full year paying tuition while I searched for a job to meet the internship requirements for school. I had to make a decision and quick. I couldn't afford to pay another year of tuition just to be enrolled. In January 2016, at five months pregnant, I found a full-time job as a therapist at a place where people cared about the population of people they served. It was perfect.

Except it wasn't. My school did not recognize my job's supervisor as a qualified supervisor, which meant I would have to pay a qualified supervisor almost half of my monthly income in order to meet the internship requirements. I felt like I had hit another wall. This time the voice to quit was louder. I couldn't quit. I had never quit anything academically in my life. I was scared and concerned about what people would say if I decided to quit.

One day I finally sat down and wrote an email to my academic advisor informing her of my decision to "withdraw from the doctoral program." My heartfelt lighter immediately after sending the email. There was a huge weight lifted from my chest. I could breathe. I continued to work as a therapist up until my maternity leave. It was after giving birth to my daughter that I started to think about my purpose in life. I knew I didn't want to be a therapist. I had long since lost my passion for it and it wasn't connected to my life's dream. As I was growing and maturing, my purpose was evolving with the choices that I was making. Purpose is not a singular gift or talent as I once thought. I've since learned that purpose is a collection of our skills, gifts, and talents that serve the higher evolution of the world.

I'd always wanted to be a writer and spent so much time writing in journals and diaries as a child, but somewhere along my life's journey, I'd lost sight of this passion. I didn't value myself or believe that anyone would want to read anything I wrote without having a Ph.D. I felt that my words didn't have value without it. It was vain to believe that having a doctorate degree would validate my intellect and self-expression. Education does not equate to intelligence. I believe this is why God didn't allow me to receive my doctorate at this point. I had to first let go of my vanity and untruths and learn to believe in myself.

After becoming a mother, I went through a huge transition, again finding myself in darkness, not knowing which direction to go. I spent almost an entire year scared of my future, as I struggled to find balance in my new roles as a wife and mom. As time went on, I knew I had to move forward. I couldn't stay stuck, wallowing in my sorrows, I may not have known exactly what to do, but I had to do something.

Lesson: Change is inevitable.

Many people are caught between who they are and the person they want to be. In this gap, there's a struggle between ego and spirit. Ego has a desire to hold on to old ways of being, doing, and thinking, while the spirit is eager to explore the abundance of possibilities that exist in a space yet to be discovered. During this time, an essential change has to occur in order to move forward.

Your foundation has to be shaken in order to create new ground and stability for upcoming change. Unfortunately, I wasn't someone that was taught how to accept change, and so whenever change occurred in my life, I refused it immensely. Some times I cried, other times I questioned and refused to move forward. I'd convinced myself that my life would always be the same, but the fact is the only thing constant in life is change. Everything you experience will change including your relationships, careers, and of course even your physical body. Nothing stays the same forever.

Life is a constant flow of changes and with change comes discomfort, chaos, and confusion. My initial reaction was to resist and ignore the change, but my unwillingness to adapt created more chaos and dysfunction. Holding on to these old ways of being, refusing to change, kept me stagnant and in a place of emptiness. You can not grow into your future Self if you're refusing to let go of your present Self.

Change is not always enjoyable and can be difficult to accept; however, change is what keeps life in motion. All of life is a result of change. Allowing the inevitable to occur in your life will shape and mold you into the version of yourself you dream about. Be willing to deepen your relationship with the changes in life. Even in the midst of chaos, trust that there is always a greater purpose.

Real change is created by those that wake up and decide to do something different. Change, both individually and collectively, is caused by a shift in foundational beliefs. That is to say, change often does not occur within the realm of comfort. You, first, have to work on yourself inwardly, creating a change in your thoughts, behaviors, and actions, and then move on to create change in your external environment.

I've come to believe that people really do not want change. As humans, it's something that we naturally avoid. We may say that we truly want different without being willing to do what it takes to create any significant change. The tactics and methods that we use for change are trivial and useless without deep commitment. We change things outwardly, like our hairstyles and our wardrobes, or our acceptance of a particular group of people, but we steer away from the depth of change that goes far beyond who we appear to be.

We condemn people for changing when we could embrace and applaud them. Often other people's change is perceived as a threat because it provides a reflection of that same ability within, though not activated as of yet. Every January when people say, "New Year, New Me," the response is belittling, condemning, and shaming. Each day we should all be striving to be better than we were the day before, not just every year. "New You" does not mean that you change just your outward appearance, it means working inwardly to change your thoughts, your behaviors, and your actions. If you are mean and surly, perhaps you will work towards being more compassionate and kind. You don't want to wake up thirty, forty, or fifty years from now with the thoughts and behaviors of your younger Self.

Be willing to step away from old beliefs about the inability to create change and really just do it. The first thing you can do to create change is ask questions. Lots of them. First to yourself and then to those around you. Secondly, you have to work to create solutions. You have to not only be willing to identify the problem, but also create the solution to the problem.

To be alive is to experience the fullness of life, to walk in your authentic truth, and to operate from a space of conscious awareness. That means to inhabit every experience that is afforded to you. New job embrace it; lose a job, embrace it. New relationship, embrace it; end of a relationship, embrace it. Every good or bad thing that you experience in life is intended for you to embrace it with the same attitude: gratefulness.

Complaining about the course of your life does not change it. In fact, doing so will keep you stagnant and held in a place that has no forward movement. Life requires that we surrender to the process of maturing. You cannot control every façade of your life. The moment you decide to let go of your perceived control, the course of your life will unfold before your eyes. Just like Dorothy's yellow brick road, the path will be paved for you and all you'll have to do is "ease on down the road."

METAMORPHOSIS

"Most people fear death. Me, I'm not afraid to die.
I've already conquered death. It's life that scares me."

~Sharon Elise~

Death has been a major teacher throughout my life. I learned at a young age that death wasn't anything to fear because it was inevitable. I still can recall Saturday morning conversations with my grandmother about her impending death. She talked about it as a matter of fact, without any emotion or feeling. This scared me. I would cry and tell her that I didn't want her to die, but she'd always say, "we are all born to die" and there was nothing I could do to change the fact that I would die one day.

To my younger self it seemed I was at a funeral what felt like every three months. This intensified my fear of death. Within a year, my uncle and father died. I was traumatized. The adults in my life didn't provide a clear understanding of death and dying: I was told that "heaven was in the sky," and that I would see my father and uncle "one day" but I really didn't understand what that meant. I started to believe everyone in my life could and would die at any moment. When my mother would go out with her girlfriends I'd stay up waiting for her to come home, fearing that something bad had happened if she wasn't home before midnight. I would repeatedly call her and her friends to make sure she was okay.

During my senior year in college, I took a "Death in Perspective" class and it was one of the best experiences of my life. As part of the course, we planned our funerals, completed a Living Will and went on several field trips to a local funeral home, the Medical Examiner's Office, and a state penitentiary. Taking this class illuminated the thin line between life and death.

On the trip to the Medical Examiner's Office, we witnessed two autopsies. We were in the same room with the human remains without any glass separating us. I saw the deceased up close and personal without the preparation given for a funeral service. The trip that sticks in my mind the most was to the state penitentiary. We visited and talked to inmates on Death Row, all of whom were imprisoned for making one choice that changed the course of their entire life.

We talked with them about their views on death and dying. One of the men said something that has stayed with me and will forever: "I have to value this breath because the next one isn't guaranteed." His statement still gives me chills. It made me think about the choices I was making in my life and how I had allowed the death of my father to have such a hold over my ability to grieve properly and heal.

On May 14, 2008, the night before I walked across the stage to receive my bachelors degree, I sat on the bathroom floor crying over the bittersweet moment that would occur the next day. The day I graduated also marked the 13th anniversary of my father's death. I didn't want to spend another year in a slumber. I decided to write a poem in his honor. After reading it aloud to myself, I took a breath and released his spirit from the bondage it had over my life. I let go. At that moment, I also let go of the fear of death. I wanted to live but I didn't really know how. I was loose but I wasn't yet set free.

Some years later, while attending a local festival in our city with my husband and daughter, I got on a roller coaster for the first time in over two years. While allowing space for excitement, I was nervous because the last time I was on a roller coaster it was a horrible experience (it was one of those rides that shoot straight up into the air and drops down really fast). I felt like my soul left my body. I was petrified. I didn't want to get on any more rides.

Something was different about this trip though. I was ready to get back out there and face my fear. This time I got on the roller coaster that swings back and forth until finally it swings all the way up, leaving riders suspended in air for what feels like forever. As I hung facing the Earth, I gazed up at the sky, taking in the blue and white hues, and I felt alive. It was at this moment I realized I was no longer afraid of death. I thought if I died at that moment, my heart is full and I'm at peace. I am not afraid to die because I know what it's like to live. I've lived many lives and died many deaths. I have lived and I am living.

That experienced also brought to mind how many times I'd transitioned between darkness and light. More times than I can count I've experienced my own death, feelings of loss and disconnection, followed by some sort of rebirth each time; knowing that no matter how far I fall into the abyss, I always can and will get back up stronger and wiser than before; grateful and thankful nonetheless to be on this side of the tunnel, where the light shines bright and I'm able to open my wings and fly.

I've always had a fascination with butterflies. In fact, one of my very first tattoos is of two butterflies joined together by their wings. This tattoo served as a reminder of one of my life's goals: to become self-actualized. According to Abraham Maslow, a world renowned psychologist, to be self-actualized is to "reach one's fullest potential." I like to think of this process as the joining of our two selves (ego and spirit) to become our True Self. I believe this is the journey of life.

Lesson: There's no sense in being scared of the inevitable.

I used to believe life was a linear process with each of us starting off as a fetus (egg) growing in our mother's womb into a baby (caterpillar), moving through life until we enter the chrysalis phase (adolescence through young adulthood), and then finally entering adulthood (butterflies), where we reach our peak and earn the right to spread our wings and fly.

I've since discovered, though, that life is not linear, it is continuous and circular. We continuously go through a metamorphosis and will continue this process throughout our lifetime. At each level of maturity (read: growth) we experience changes in our behavior, thoughts, and actions. We essentially die of our old selves to become a 'new' self. We awaken to a new level of understanding than our previous self was aware of or could comprehend. We are continuously changing from caterpillar to chrysalis to butterfly.

Caterpillar

As a caterpillar we are unaware of the metamorphosis process. This is our feeding stage. We gain knowledge, insight, and perspective through our experiences, interactions, and relationships with other caterpillars. We are learning and growing during this stage - making caterpillar friends and enjoying our caterpillar lives.

We move through life as and are content with being caterpillars. We do not know that our life as a caterpillar will soon come to an end and that we will be transformed into one of the most beautiful creatures in the world. We are unaware of the other life that is awaiting us.

Chrysalis

Caterpillars instinctively reach higher ground to find a twig or a leaf to become a pupa. This process is known as chrysalis. To the caterpillar, seemingly their life is coming to an end. It may not look like anything is happening but a lot of changes are taking place on the inside. During this phase the caterpillar grows new legs, eyes, and even wings! All of this takes place in darkness, alone, high-up and away from others. The space is tight, the caterpillar can't move and senses that life has come to an end. At this stage the caterpillar no longer exists. The caterpillar dies of itself and is transformed into a butterfly.

During this phase of our life we experience great tragedy. Think of the chrysalis process as going through a valley. We face many trials and tribulations, obstacles, and struggles. Life appears to be unfair and every turn seems to be the wrong turn. Nothing goes as planned and we become uncertain about the direction of our life. We do not yet know that everything we are experiencing is preparing us for something greater. When we go through hardships in life, we become frustrated, angry, and upset. Like the caterpillar, we do not know that we are experiencing a transformation. We feel defeated, doubtful, and hopeless. All the pain, heartache, and struggle is preparing us for the next phase of our life. We are growing new legs, eyes, and wings so that once we break out of our chrysalis we can learn how to fly.

Butterfly

What emerges from the chrysalis, is a scared and yet beautiful butterfly. Though the butterfly now has wings, it is incapable of flying just yet. In order for the butterfly to use what it has been given during the metamorphosis process, it has to wait for its wings to dry. If the butterfly attempts to fly before its wings are ready, it could fall to its death.

After going through difficult times in our life, we spring up as new beings, filled with greater energy, gusto, and faith than we did before. There is a greater sense of hope, faith, and determination that we can do anything that we put our minds to. As butterflies we are capable of taking on the world. We've gained knowledge through our metamorphosis that we will use in our new life as butterflies. Though we've gained useful knowledge and insight, we may not be able to use it right away.

Isn't it frustrating when you've been given valuable information and/or tools, but still do not have the capability to use what has been given to you? This preparation period is extremely important! We must trust the process and our place in life's endless cycle. Soon we will be capable of taking flight without any resistance or struggle.

Everything in nature has the perfect timing. Whether you are a caterpillar, chrysalis, or butterfly, trust the timing of the space you are in. Soon you will be transformed from who you think you are into someone you never imagined you could be. Like a caterpillar, you will evolve from something small and simple into something vibrant and beautiful. We are all caterpillars transitioning into butterflies and back again. There's growth in every phase of our life, show gratitude and appreciation for where you are and trust the process. We are all in transition.

O' YE OF LITTLE FAITH

"Faith is taking the first step even when you don't see
the staircase."

~Rev. Dr. Martin Luther King, Jr.~

Three. The number of times I strongly considered
committing suicide. Each time more intense than the
previous attempt. My body would become
immobilized by the intensity of pain I felt. I hadn't
yet learned healthy coping mechanisms to deal with
pain so each time I was met with a hardship, my
thoughts became negative followed by my behavior.

With each visit to the abyss, the level of pain became more unbearable.

The first time I thought about suicide was the night my father died. Since I was seven and hadn't developed an emotionally healthy response to pain, I didn't want to live without my father; I couldn't imagine a world where he didn't exist. So I went into the bathroom and started banging my head on the bathtub. I was crying so hard wanting the pain to end that my mother eventually broke into the bathroom and held me tight. I wonder if she knew this would be a heavy burden I'd have to bear. She bore it with me as best she could.

The second time occurred much later during my senior year of college. I spent four years in self inquiry and yet again found myself in the middle of drama a few months before graduation. I was caught up in emptiness, pain, and again attached to people who I thought could fill the void. I was completely confused about how to get out of that vicious cycle.

The final time I considered suicide, during graduate school working on my Master's degree, was the lowest point and most serious attempt: instead of just thoughts, I had a plan. I was too overwhelmed with no relief insight and wanted out. While managing an 18-credit course load, working two part-time jobs, dealing with family stress, an unhealthy relationship, and smack in the middle of my two-year program, my life came tumbling down. It was almost as if God was saying, I will not allow you to move forward with any of this baggage anymore.

I refused to allow the enemy to hold me captive to something that I did not believe. I would not be defined by my family, a failed relationship or anything outside of myself. At that moment, I decided to return to God. I don't know what it was, but something inside was demanding that I wake up. On December 7, 2011, I made my way to Christian Love Baptist Church in Irvington, NJ and gave my life to Christ. This had been my third time returning to church, but this time was different. As they say, "third times the charm."

As the late great, Dr. Ronald B. Christian began the altar call, I walked to the front of the church, eyes filled with tears and fell to my knees. I had returned home ready to atone and ask for forgiveness. I was ready to commit my life to God and His works instead of my own selfish desires. I knew whatever I would face in life, whatever I was up against, I couldn't do it alone. It was in that moment I knew without a shadow of a doubt, God was in control and my faith, though as small as a mustard seed, had gotten me through.

There were times in my life I delayed making choices for myself because I believed the people in my life were capable, willing, and able to make better choices for me. I'd placed my future in the hands of others and when they left me feeling disappointed, ashamed, and abused, I'd do nothing. Instead I would take the beating and be left with not so much as a float to keep my head above water.

I was giving to others what I ultimately hadn't given to myself. I lacked faith in myself and was hoping, praying, even begging for others to have faith in me; faith that I would be a better person, that I could love, and that I could heal from my father's death.

The problem was that I couldn't trust myself so how could I expect anyone else to trust me? I had been very impulsive and reckless in my decision-making in relationships, friendships, and career choices, confusing my heart with my emotions.

During those times of struggle, I lost sight of my faith and purpose. I would give in to fear and doubt, feeling defeated and ready to give up on life. I had to let go of my attachments to the people in my life and learn to put my faith in myself and God. I had to get up and keep moving forward. The more I was capable of going with the flow, the more I was able to exercise my faith during those low moments.

I am still in the process of learning to trust myself. Now when I'm faced with a hardship, though I still seek outside counsel when needed, ultimately I am able to make healthier decisions because I've learned to trust myself and my ability to make the best decisions for my life.

Lesson: *Your faith (or lack thereof) creates your circumstances.*

In life, there are peaks and valleys. We ebb and flow between the two throughout our lifespan. The peaks in your life are moments of celebration for the work you've put in. It's a time to rejoice and to enjoy the happiness of the moment because it is only a moment. With every peak, there is a valley waiting for you around the corner.

Your valley moments are humbling experiences that remind you of the struggles of life. They present a trial for you to overcome in order to reach a much higher peak. When dark clouds appear, be like an eagle and fly through the storm. The darkness does not ever go away but your relationship to it changes: there is always light on the other side. You will have the ability to overcome it in order to continue your walk towards greatness.

There's no clear map for the journey of life. There will be many ups and downs, an array of different emotions, some good times, some bad. Through it all, you must keep moving. Regardless of the number of times life knocks you down, what matters most is that you get back up. You are stronger than anything life brings your way.

Life comes with many difficult situations, like the death of a loved one, loss of a job, the end of a relationship, or financial difficulties. These are all experiences that do not elicit positive feelings and often times, it's hard to be optimistic when you're experiencing a hardship.

We all experience hardships in our lives. No one is invisible and thus capable of escaping the harsh realities that come along with this beautiful nightmare we call life. Though you will face different challenges and obstacles along the way, you must remain dedicated and committed to your path. Often times we allow life obstacles to prevent us from pushing forward.

When we have a clear and harmonious relationship with our emotions, they are the best advisors, however, the sad truth is we've been miseducated about emotions. Having a disharmonious relationship with your emotions will lead you to making permanent decisions with temporary feelings. When you become capable of listening and trusting your emotions, a world of peace is created for you. The peace you will have in your heart is better than any worry, anxiety, or fear that you've ever had. It feels good to be able to trust yourself. Trusting your spirit allows you the space to say, "I know what's best for me" and to be able to stand behind that conviction.

You have to trust that you are capable of making the best decision for yourself when things seem difficult and you find yourself at a crossroad. You have to gain trust for yourself. Trust in your abilities, your thinking, your choices, and in your behaviors. In those moments when you don't know which way to go, stand still, breathe deeply, exhale, and move towards your spirit, trusting and knowing that the decisions you make is ultimately the best you can make for yourself.

This will require stepping outside of your comfort zone and challenging yourself to face your fears. One of my favorite quotes comes from Iyanla Vanzant, she says, "Go towards that which makes you most uncomfortable because that's the only way you will grow." This requires sitting with your discomfort in order to evolve beyond it.

When things seem tough, know that you are a conqueror and already have all the strength you need to complete any task that comes your way. The choices and decisions you make today will have a direct impact on your tomorrow. Put your faith in action.

FORGIVENESS

"It's one of the greatest gifts you can give yourself, to forgive. Forgive everybody."

~Maya Angelou~

Forgiveness was the hardest lesson for me to learn. I used to be "Queen of Grudges" and wore that crown proudly. It would take a long time for me to forgive anyone I felt had wronged or hurt me in any way. I didn't recognize that my inability to forgive was a sign of anger and animosity. I carried around the baggage of hurt and pain for so long because I was angry with so many people: my father, my mother, but mostly with myself.

As I was preparing to move to Massachusetts, I stopped by my pastor's office to seek guidance in securing a church home in my new town. I shared my plans for ways I wanted to be of service in the church once I completed my degree and returned home. As I was rambling on and on about the ways I wanted to give back, I noticed a puzzled look on his face. He interjected and said, "It sounds like you are trying to swim across the ocean with cinder blocks."

It was a moment of revelation. His intuitive nature provided the clearest reflection of where I was in my life at that time. Holding on to weight from my past while trying to embrace the prospect of the future. I had to be willing to let go of the baggage that was weighing me down and that was starting to take affect on me emotionally and mentally. I had to do the work to heal from the traumas of my past. This would require an internal process of travel through the mind to explore the places of brokenness and pain.

My lack of apathy towards the world and everyone in it rendered me helpless, hopeless, and faithless. I had to atone for my sins. I had to ask for forgiveness, first of myself and then to those that I'd wronged or hurt in any way. I wanted to be set free.

I spent an entire year working on forgiveness. Moving to Massachusetts, provided the perfect opportunity for solitude. I spent most of my time in my apartment alone. It was perhaps one of the most depressing times of my life, but it provided the space for me to find myself. I got to decide who I wanted to be. I also got to see how the world viewed me, free from my comfort zone and away from anything familiar. I was in the wild.

Once again, taking the time to improve my self awareness, I started reading self-help books, journaling, and learning more about spirituality. I discovered some negative patterns of behavior, like saying I wanted things to be better without doing anything to change my circumstances. I recognized that I really didn't like the person I had become. I had to forgive myself for all the seemingly bad choices I'd made.

It was at this point I discovered I could not go forward without releasing all that had been weighing me down. I had to let go of the guilt, shame, fear, doubt, and other low vibrating emotions no longer serving my higher purpose. I had to forgive myself for all I'd blamed myself for. I was broken and as a result, I was hateful and hurtful to the people in my life and to myself. I had a lot of broken relationships that needed mending.

After I cleared up my issues within myself, I wrote a letter to my father. I had a lot of things I'd always wished I could say to him, and blame I felt he should take responsibility for. In the four-page letter, I wrote about my disappointment with the choices he made that ultimately lead to his death. I cried, I prayed, then burned the letter after I was done. It was one of the most healing experiences that has yet to occur in my life. I felt an instant sense of peace. I was free.

After writing the letter to my father, I took a trip back home to New Jersey to visit my mother. I wanted to let her know how I felt about my upbringing and choices she'd made that I'd blamed her for. As a child, she and I always bumped heads, mostly because I thought I knew everything. I was hard-headed, selfish and disrespectful towards my mother over the years and hadn't valued her for all the sacrifices she'd made for me. I forgave my mother realizing she did the best she could; this quickly mended our relationship and we started being able to communicate better. Though I may not have agreed with all of them, I pay homage for every choice that she made. I'm grateful for my mother for the service of her spirit and for helping me become the woman I am today.

I continued my atonement by asking relatives, friends, and foes for their forgiveness. I wanted to clear my slate. I could not move forward in my journey with the sorrows of yesterday weighing me down. I wasn't expecting any apologies in return or even felt one was needed. I needed to completely release myself from the energy of my past behaviors and choices. I was asking for forgiveness for me. Forgiveness is not for the other person, it is for you. It's about being able to release the anger and move on from it instead of carrying it.

Being in a new city where I didn't know anyone gave me a lot of time to reflect. I spent so much time in my apartment crying and feeling ashamed of myself and my past. I asked God for forgiveness daily as I committed to working on forgiveness within myself and with the people in my life. After the year was completed, I finally felt ready to move forward. I had asked forgiveness from every person I could, I had completed the work of atonement. My soul was renewed.

Lesson: Forgiveness is the gateway to the soul.

Forgiveness is extremely important as you enter into the next phase of your journey. If you are not willing to forgive or ask for forgiveness it can become cancerous to your being. There is power in atoning because even when others have wronged you in some way, there's much you can accept responsibility for too.

Forgiveness is not one-sided. We all have something that we can be accountable for, even if it is just apologizing for holding on to anger. Forgive yourself and watch the weight be lifted from your chest. While it's easier to accept emotions like joy, laughter, and happiness as opposed to sentiments like anger, frustration, and sadness, through the process of forgiveness we free ourselves of carrying that burden at all.

No one person is to blame for your life being the way that it is right now. If you are not at peace, then search your heart for areas where you can forgive and let go. Your life will never be better than it is now unless you choose to let go of anything working against your forward mobility.

We create more pain and chaos for ourselves by holding on to emotions that do not serve the greatest evolution of our Self. When we acknowledge our emotions, accept them for what they are, and allow them to pass through, we can enter into the next experience with complete awareness. In order to have complete awareness of your journey, you'll have to enter free of your attachment to the past; you'll have to open yourself up to forgiveness.

Life will call you to make some difficult choices. You'll have to let go of some people, places, and things: the hate for your father, the resentment towards your mother, the distrust of your partner, and the guilt of your past. The longer you allow it to take up space in your life, the harder it will be for you to move ahead. As Pastor Ron told me, "you can't swim across the ocean with cinder blocks."

Guilt cannot reside where forgiveness lays; there is no shame where there is love; there is no doubt where there is faith. The natural cycle of life does not permit us to remain in one spot. All of life is about evolution and growth. The only state of being that that has lasting effects is peace. Peace is a state of balance from which you cannot be distracted or disturbed. When you are at true peace, regardless of what is happening around you, you are capable of withstanding any force that comes against you.

Consider for a moment that the things you've been holding on to are the very things preventing you moving forward along your journey. Seek peace through forgiveness and watch as God moves in great ways to support the changes in your life. The process of your healing begins through your ability to forgive yourself and others. Begin the work to heal yourself from the inside and that process will affect the outside. Then search your heart and see if there is anyone you need to forgive or ask for forgiveness.

Release it. Let it go. Forgive them and then forgive yourself. Your peace will follow.

LOVE FOR ONE'S SELF

"Self-love has very little to do with
how you feel about your outer self. It's about
accepting all of yourself."

~Tyra Banks~

One of my close friends started a blog before blogging became popular. I remember reading her blog posts and feeling so inspired. I asked her if I could be a guest blogger once and she said yes. I wrote a blog post entitled, *A Single Girl's Guide to Dating 101*. In this blog post, I wrote about the importance of being whole before entering into a relationship because "you can't love anyone else until

82

you [are whole within] yourself." The sad truth is I wasn't even close to living this life. I had all the wisdom, but no action on the matter.

I succumbed to the mediocre ideals of love because I hadn't yet experienced the fullness of it. I meaninglessly used the term and reduced its power to a simple word instead of an experience. I created a subjective view of love and my expression of it varied depending on the various dynamics that affected my feelings during that time. I was not effectively expressing the true nature of love because I was unfamiliar with it. I was pouring an unconditional, unapologetic love into other people, but wasn't giving it to myself.

When I met my husband he showed me a different side of myself. He and I met during a time where I was completely out of sync. I was unemployed, living with my mother, and basically trying to figure out where my life was heading. During our first meeting, I shared my struggles about being unemployed for over year, and it was his response that caught my attention: "you have allowed something cancerous to take over your mind and you can't think clearly." I thought "Whoa, okay. Who is this guy!?" After dating for about two months, we knew we wanted to spend the rest of our lives together. It was something we just felt, not only in our heart space, but also in our intuition. It was this magical feeling all over any time we connected. We had found love.

The thing about love, though, is that you have to contain it otherwise it can be explosive. My husband has reflected some hard truths and we've experienced some challenging times, chaos and madness in our marriage, but through it all we grow from it and we are able to do the work to make each other better. Iron sharpens iron. He helps me to see that I'm not perfect, and yet I'm whole in my imperfection.

Marriage was another opportunity for me to deepen my self-love. To love oneself requires the commitment to extend beyond our own desires to support the nourishment and growth of not only ourselves but also those whom we are connected to. Until then, the love I had for myself was surface-level and hadn't reached the level of practicality. One day while looking in the mirror, I thought, "Sharon, you don't love yourself, if you did you'd be more disciplined in your word." I was writing about the importance of having faith and belief in one's self, though I wasn't practicing this truth in my own life. If I truly believed in myself, I would have been putting my faith into action, instead I was judging myself and living in fear.

I hadn't truly loved myself because it wasn't something that was taught to me. I was taught to accept a version of myself that was pleasing to the people in my environment. How could I love the parts of myself that were mean, unkind, and hurtful? I wanted to bury those aspects of myself without any further thought. Prior to lessons learned in love, I refused to see myself through any lens other than perfection.

Lack of self-awareness is dangerous and is a reflection of one's lack of self-love. I had to learn to accept all of me, without judgment or shame, owning who I am, and accepting the good with the bad without making any excuses.

Lesson: The love you give yourself is the love you give to the world.

Love is the greatest substance on this planet. It has the power to create, heal, and transform. It is by far the most powerful superpower the human race will ever know. Though it is very much a part of our daily lives, many people do not have an in-depth understanding of what love truly is. Love is more than the physical and emotional stimulation you receive from another person. Love goes far beyond the things that anyone can do for you.

Most people in the world, when asked what they want in life reply, "To be happy." Though there may be some level of uncertainty surrounding the details of what happiness looks like, we are certain to strive for this state of being. We fluctuate in and out of moments of happiness based on our experiences and the sensations we feel from being stimulated by those experiences. We then equate these moments into our understanding of what it means to be happy.

The richest people in the world are generally the least happy while the most impoverished people in the world have a tremendous capacity to experience true happiness. Yet we still equate time, money, and success with happiness. Materialism and tangible things have become representations of our level of happiness. We believe we'll be happier upon attaining a certain level of success, money, or power. Happiness is an emotional state of being and like all emotions it is fleeting.

The true nature of love is a representation of an experience, not just a feeling. It is an experience that many people find hard to even describe. It fills the atmosphere with heightening energy that allows us to show compassion, care, and kindness to one another. In his book, *The Road Less Travelled*, M. Scott Peck defines love as "the will to extend one's self for the purpose of nurturing one's own or another's spiritual growth." It is an unwavering commitment to the challenges and struggles of life, not only for yourself, but to everyone whom you're connected to that you love – all with the intention to grow and evolve.

Self-love is the highest form of love that we can experience. It is not conceited or arrogant, but requires self-awareness, self-knowledge, and self-discipline. Self-love is the willingness to accept the wholeness of who you are. Self-love cannot be attained. Every day you have to make a commitment to love yourself, wholly, freely, and boldly as you are. When you make a mistake, love yourself; if you judge someone, love yourself; failed relationship or no relationship, love yourself. Self-love is a daily cognitive process that takes place within your being. It says, "whatever happens to me today, good, bad, or indifferent, I'm still the best version of myself and am worthy of love."

You will always have areas where improvements can be made. You must be willing to become an expert of your Self. You'll hold yourself back by refusing to learn the lesson the first time around and then find yourself repeating the same situations over and over again. Though the circumstances may differ, the cycle remains the same until the lesson is learned.

You cannot give to others what you have yet to give to yourself. There needs to be a balance between selfishness and selflessness. Love of self is immensely important to life's journey; however, if it is true in nature it will never be at the expense of hurting anyone else. The relationships you have in your life are intended to teach you lessons about who you are.

I shared with my mother once that she's been my greatest teacher. Imagine my surprise when she replied that I'd been hers too. Even in parental relationships, children teach parents valuable life lessons. In every relationship in our life, we are simultaneously teachers and students.

Collectively we need a shift in our understanding of love. Starting within to raise the collective experience of love, it then spreads widely and deeply throughout the Universe. Love yourself, first, then share and spread love to others. Your first experience of love was inside your mother's womb before you'd ever physically met her, you loved her. This is the passion and depth of the love you need to share with the world; without cause and without expectation of return.

Spend some time today reflecting on the areas of growth in your life. Ask yourself, "What is it that I can do to improve the quality of my life and relationships?" Hold yourself accountable. It is up to you to strengthen and cultivate a positive and meaningful life. Become a student in life's class. The subject is all about you. Take notes. There's much to learn about who you really are!

FACING FEAR

"Some people look before they leap, others just leap."

~Kris Marlene~

It is amazing how some people seem to be born fearless. It's as if they can, and often will, do anything without it giving them the slightest inclination of fear. They are spontaneous and adventurous. They run towards the things they fear with an awareness and an intuitive knowing of their ability to conquer what's in front of them. While this may be true for some people, it's not the case for everyone. I am not someone that is fearless, in fact, I'd say I was very much fear-filled, often times living in a constant state of fear: fear of the unknown, other people, and even myself. I found myself holding my breath during every new encounter, uncertain of myself and unaware of the disconnection between myself and the fear I felt.

On a plane back home to New Jersey from Atlanta once, I noticed I didn't like not having the ability to see when the plane was landing. Normally during plane rides, I request the window seat; however, during this trip, I'd given up my beloved window seat so a family of three could sit together.

Not only did I not have a window seat, but the person sitting in the window seat in our row had the shade closed. I was terrified as the plane prepared for landing. I noticed my mind racing, thinking of all the terrible things that could happen: What if the plane didn't land safely? What if we crashed?

On the drive home, I reflected on that moment of not seeing the plane landing and realized I would experience this level of fear quite often when I didn't have control over a situation. I assumed the worst in any situation outside of my control and I wanted to change this rigid mindset. I wanted to be able to expect the best or at the very least change my mindset to be present without experiencing racing thoughts.

I recognized the power of thoughts. I knew if I was thinking negatively over and over again, I was unconsciously drawing negative experiences into my life. I knew if I could control my thoughts, just by shifting my mindset from negative to positive, I would be able to attract positive energy in my life. Essentially this positive energy would overflow into my relationships, finances, and health. I needed to make a change.

This took quite some time and happened in small increments over time. I started facing smaller fears and then gradually worked towards facing bigger fears. I'd thought because I'd faced one fear I'd be able to conquer the next fear easily. I learned quickly every fear isn't created equal. Each time I'd have to muster up strength to move beyond fear.

I didn't want to remain stagnant, scared of life's challenges, refusing to grow into the best version of myself. I knew that if I wanted to free myself from the unrealistic fears of my mind, I had to work hard to gain strength, confidence, and endurance in order to conquer my fears.

At times I'll still feel anxiety in my chest when I'm faced with a fear. I bring awareness to the feeling, breathe deeply, and do it anyway, thinking "What's the worst that can happen?" Often, I can't think of anything too horrible that's worth not proceeding. I also, ask myself, "What's the best that can happen?" This type of thinking has allowed me to be fully present and more engaged with life.

I don't allow fear to create a narrative for me when I can create one for myself. I choose how I want to move forward. I own my future and although fear may be present instead of being in front of me as a constant reminder of what I can't get over, it's behind me as a reminder of what I've overcome.

Lesson: Fear and faith cannot exist in the same space.

It is a courageous act to step outside of your comfort zone to feel the discomfort of your fears. You'll face storms, endure pain, and it will all appear to be too unbearable. The traumatic experiences of life seem to make it impossible to remain committed to the journey. During these times you may feel depleted, beat down, hopeless, and disconnected, incapable of seeing the light at the end of the tunnel.

Fear can show up in many ways. Any situation that causes you to respond with "fight, freeze, or flight" is rooted in the energy of fear. When you choose to fight, you respond to life circumstances in whatever manner they show up. Whether it be a negative or positive experience, your response is to take action to respond to life and the integrity of your response will determine the trajectory of your path.

Any response that results in stagnation or depletion is a freeze response. The inability to react to the trauma and suffering that appears in your life is a restrictive response to fear. It does not provide growth or forward mobility; however can be beneficial. Often times in the face of fear, one might be inclined to be destructive to personal or public property or make unhealthy choices that do not produce forward movement. In these moments, the best response is to be still and do nothing. In the face of fear, no response is better than an unhealthy one. Unhealthy choices can, and often do lead to further decay, chaos, and discomfort.

The last response to fear is to remove yourself from it, to take flight or flee. Although this may seem to be an inadequate response, there are times and situations that call for a release or submitting to fear to provide both a humbling and elevating experience. This response provides the space for the energy of fear to dissipate until an appropriate response can be made. It's appropriate to flee from fear when you do not have the health, sanity, or willpower to push forward. It's imperative for you to seek solace and counsel to return to an optimal state of being. Facing fear in the midst of chaos will prove to be damaging to your health, both mentally and spiritually. There will be times when you will need to retreat – this does not equate to defeat.

When facing fear, you'll have to develop discernment of the appropriate responses to make. There are times when fleeing may be the best choice and others times when it is not. Learning to exercise your inner wisdom during these moments will prove to be victorious. No matter what fears you face, you will conquer them; maybe with tears in your eyes, a little bruised, or a little scarred, but you will survive.

Fear can be healthy if you choose to use it to your benefit: let your fear work for you instead of against you. Free yourself from fear of the past, fear of the future, or any other fear blocking you from growing into your best self. The next time fear shows up, ask yourself, "What is causing me to feel this way?" You'll find by bringing yourself to the present moment you can acknowledge your feelings and consciously choose to face your fear head on.

Once you know what is causing your fear, you are capable of moving past it. So when you are faced with another fear, (because you will, again and again, and again) then you will be able to recall your previous victories and prepare for what's ahead. You'll approach uncertainties with strength and conviction, being stronger and wiser because you've already overcome previous fears. Regardless of how fear shows up in your life, trust and know that you will prevail. Victory is the conquering moment. This is freedom.

I read on a fortune cookie once, "It's not the strong but the responsive that survive." Respond to your fear instead of allowing it to keep you caged in, holding you back from walking boldly into your future. Break free of the cage, move past your fear, and walk into the greatness that awaits you.

BELIEVE IN YOURSELF

"As we let our own light shine, we unconsciously give other people permission to do the same."

~Marianne Williamson~

When I was younger I loved to sing. Although I didn't have the best singing voice, there was something freeing about using my voice to create music. I loved it. I'd sing at parties, in the car during road trips, in the shower, and was in the choir in elementary school. I'd sing where ever and whenever I felt like it. I didn't care that I didn't sound as good as Beyoncé or Mariah. I loved the way singing made me feel. Until I stopped. All throughout my childhood I was told how horrible my voice was. Not just my singing voice, even my speaking voice was deemed "annoying and whiny" by family members and friends. Whenever I would sing around my house, my grandmother would profess, "you sound like someone stepping on a cat."

At different points during my life, the same message was echoed in various ways from family members and friends. "You sound terrible, please stop." I started to believe my voice didn't matter, therefore I didn't matter, and I started treating myself like I didn't. For so many years, this was my pattern of behavior.

My mother encouraged me to use my voice, but mostly when it was pleasing to her and the other adults in my life. Whenever I shared something that I believed to be my truth, it was met with aggression, shot down or dismissed. This caused me to believe and accept other peoples' truth, instead of discovering my own beliefs and values, I adopted those of my family and friends.

I hadn't yet developed the capacity to trust my Self and listen to my inner voice, my inner guide. I was moving so fast through life, racing towards an ending that I wasn't quite sure of. Once I'd stopped to reflect on my behaviors I was able to see that I was erratic. I experienced really high highs followed by really low lows. There were some days I was just melancholy.

The lessons I'd learned thus far provided discernment in order to move forward. There were times when I wanted to lay around in bed, wallowing in my sorrows, choosing to complain about the circumstances of my life, but that wouldn't change anything. I had to take action. I had to learn to trust my Self and my instincts.

This required an immense amount of healing, self-care, and soul work. I created my first self-care practice at twenty-five, after discovering Iyanla Vanzant's self-help books. Reading her books provided a sense of connectivity that I'd never experienced in any of the previous books I'd read. Her books were so vulnerable, enlightening, and inspiring.

In addition to my journaling practice, I started meditating and practicing yoga. I noticed significant changes in my emotional and mental well-being. I also felt a deeper sense of connection with God. Though I started a self-care practice, maintaining it wasn't easy. A series of valley moments continued to occur intermittently throughout my life causing a shift in the balance I'd previously established.

Suddenly, instead of being rooted with my feet planted to the ground, I felt as if I was being pushed off a cliff, tumbling down, uncertain if I'd survive the fall. Each time I found myself in a downward spiral, losing focus and balance, feeling depressed, struggling to catch my breath, and without any knowledge of the trajectory of my path.

During these valley moments, I lacked discipline in my self-care practice and would choose to continue falling. Instead of responding to life's circumstances I'd freeze and succumb to them, causing further fear or doubt to surface amidst the chaos.

The ability to focus on the present moment provided the opportunity to bring awareness to the onset of a valley before it began: I would experience a shift in my emotions, usually based on some external factor, fear would show up and I'd refuse to take any action. Instead I'd find myself, yet again, stuck in a vicious cycle of stagnation, that is, until I learned it was my disbelief in my ability to move forward that was creating those patterns.

During a phone conversation with a good friend, she stopped me to say, "You have a very powerful voice." This blew me away. No one had ever complimented or said anything remotely positive about my voice. After constantly being told how annoying and whiny my voice was, I started to believe it. I would even experience extreme levels of discomfort when I'd leave voicemails, only choosing to do so when absolutely necessary. Most times I'd opt out.

I stopped singing because I didn't believe in the power of my voice. I allowed the opinions of others to keep me from expressing myself freely, losing my authentic voice in the process. I hadn't realized that I also minimized talking, on a conscious level at least. I wasn't talking about the things that matter: my true feelings, how I felt hurt, scared, and broken, how there were days, weeks, even months I'd go without shedding a tear, how I felt as if I carried the weight of the world on my back.

If my friend hadn't said something positive about my voice, I wonder if my perspective would have changed. I'm glad she gave me a new outlook about my voice because now I'm using it. One day while driving in the car, I played an old, cherished playlist and sang my heart out. It felt good to release sound and sing, though off tune, but still singing because it was my song to sing. I set myself free. Free from the cage I'd made for myself. I knew in that moment my voice matters. My thoughts matter. My beliefs matter. I matter.

Lesson: Your belief in yourself determines the outcome of your future.

Imagine a world where you are the only person that held your beliefs and values, everyone else is opposed to the fundamental values you hold as truth. People do not treat each other with love, respect, and compassion and are expected to compete with one another to advance their own individual needs. Can you imagine a world like this? Would you still hold true to your values although you would be viewed as an outsider and shunned for having different beliefs?

Certain things hold great value to who we are because we are taught and conditioned that they are true. If you were born into a Christian family system, you did not celebrate and observe Ramadan or Hanukkah; most likely you and your family observed holidays like Christmas and Easter. The things that we are taught hold great value to who we are and the beliefs and values that we hold to be true.

Standing for something that you value is not an easy feat; even if you aren't the only person who believes in it, it requires great strength and confidence. We live in a world where we are ridiculed for taking the road less travelled. We are expected to fall in to line, while our character, sanity, and well-being is often threatened because of our decision to be our authentic self.

Not everyone will support you or hold the same belief as you. You have to display a heightened sense of integrity and commitment to your beliefs, withstanding any opposition that will come (because it will come, in many forms). Even your family, friends, partner, etc. will exercise their doubts in your beliefs. Stand firm anyway. You were born to stand out. People will come against you for having different thoughts, ideas, and opinions; however you shouldn't let this sway you from holding on to your truth.

You may find yourself looking externally for motivation and encouragement; however you are capable of tapping into that small, hidden place that only you have access to for strength. From this inner place, you can remember who you are and what you've been called to do in this lifetime. Your gift of discernment gives you the capability to make progressive choices to move you further along your path once you've aligned with your purpose.

It is your divine purpose to spread light in a world full of darkness. Exposing your light to lower frequencies can have a negative impact on the luminance of your light. Most often we do not believe what we cannot see. You have to believe in your life's calling even if no one sees the vision you have for your future. Sometimes this will mean standing alone in a crowd to fight for the cause. This is how leaders are born. Leaders choose to do something different while everyone else is content with being and acting the same. It takes nothing to join the crowd. It takes everything to stand alone.

This does not take away from the feelings of sadness, hurt, or depression during the valley moments. Life is hard and can be difficult. It's okay to experience negative emotions and not want to think about the positive side of things; however, avoid staying in a space of negativity. Anytime I find myself in this space, I know that I have to move forward. Scared, uncertain, but progressing nonetheless.

Have you continued to make the same choices over and over again without positive results? Are you on the path of least resistance or stuck in a repetitive cycle of unrecognized potential? Life is all about the choices we make. You can continue to make the same choices expecting different results or you can take steps in the direction you want to create for your life. Choose to do something different that will lead you to places you have yet to discover. This is the beginning of belief in yourself. Your future is waiting for you to create it. It takes a great deal of courage to know your purpose and to walk in that resolve, especially in the presence of fear.

DISTRACTIONS

Do not be conformed to this world, but be
transformed by the renewal of your mind, that by
testing you may discern what is the will of God,
what is good and acceptable and perfect.
~Romans 12:2, *English Standard Version*~

I thought I'd reached a point in my life, where I'd
overcome enough challenges to move forward and
remain steadfast on the journey. Yet I found myself,
yet again, caught in a vicious cycle unsure of how to
see my way out. This time the culprit was
distractions. I experience so much joy and peace
when I am present, enjoying the moment, yet

somehow my attention is often drawn towards other things.

I find my thoughts racing from one point to the next, consumed by past events or future visions, but never fully present in the moment. This creates extreme levels of anxiety, discomfort, and lack of focus. To operate at full capacity, I needed to become more disciplined with my time and attention. The problem was distractions were literally everywhere and kept my attention and focus on everything except the present moment.

Knowing this I had to become more aware of myself and the things I was giving my attention to. I am easily distracted and it can be hard for me to enter stillness and focus on one thing at times like when I want to rest, be creative, or play with my daughter – my thoughts begin racing and block my awareness of the present moment. Instead, I welcome the opportunity to divert my attention for a brief moment of pleasure or satisfaction. I wasn't placing my priorities high on my to-do list and instead chose to succumb to every distraction that came with an invitation of enjoyment and entertainment.

If I was going to eliminate these behaviors and thoughts, I had to improve my awareness of them. This required recognition and acceptance of several unhealthy habits and behaviors, such as noticing the feelings of lethargy, depression, and sadness any time I was faced with fear. Instead of taking action to eliminate or minimize the distractions, I cowered in my shell refusing to do anything about them.

Writing a book is nothing like the academic papers I had to write in college, where I'd wait until the night before, cramming and writing frantically to complete the assignment to turn in the next morning. This essentially was my modus operandi in college (and during high school too): waiting until the last minute to complete assignments.

In those moments of haste and pressure, I was able to create some of my best work and received decent grades on the assignments. That's how I learned to complete work, under great pressure, at the last minute, and without structure or discipline.

What happened once I became more intentional and purposeful with my time was both perplexing and difficult to overcome. It seemed the more focused I'd become, the more distractions increased. As I struggled to remain dedicated to my goals, an opposing energy was working overtime to take my attention away. Sometimes I wanted to quit and questioned if it was worth continuing. Then I remembered life is a series of peaks and valleys.

While things may seem tumultuous and chaotic, I could not allow the distractions to stop me. This required an evaluation and elimination of the distractions that were showing up in my life. I took notice of the things I was giving my time and attention to that were keeping me away from accomplishing my goals.

My cell phone was a huge distraction. I would spend more time on my iPhone than I care to mention. I'd find any reason to have it in my hand, for text messaging and emails or to play games or for social media or to play music. Although it was always on silent to avoid obsessively running to it whenever I received a notification, this had very little effect as I'd end up checking for notifications often. I had to break-up with my phone to regain focus and continue to work towards my goals. I also had to minimize the amount of time I spent watching television. Now, when I accomplish a goal, I reward myself by binge-watching a few shows before getting back to work.

Things weren't the only distractions that were taking my attention away from my goals, people were distracting me too. Whenever someone called and took up too much of my time or when I was left feeling drained or depleted, I took notice. I started to disconnect from the people in my life that had become detrimental to my ability to stay focused and on task.

Anything or anyone that was not supportive of my higher purpose, I eliminated or at the very least minimized my interaction and exchange of energy. It required a lot of hard work, commitment, and discipline to remain focused and dedicated, all characteristics I was lacking when I first started my journey.

Anytime I sat down to start working on this book, there would be a distraction, whether it was my thoughts racing, the phone ringing or simple lack of will, I couldn't manage to cross "complete book" from my to-do list. Instead, I'd start working on something else that required less focus and more creativity. If I expected to accomplish my goal and complete this book, I would have to focus and stay committed to getting it done. This book wasn't going to write itself. The work would never get done if every time I started writing, my commitment and dedication wave.

There were many days I was doubtful and uncertain if I had the willpower to write a book. After two months without making so much as a dent in the book, I had an epiphany. I asked myself, "How important is it for you to get this book done?" I thought, "Very important." That was all I needed. I sat down to create a timeline of hours that I would dedicate to working on it. I set a goal, started working towards it, and ultimately got it done. Still, it was not as simple as creating a plan, working towards it, and "poof" the book was magically written.

The fact is I set a date, missed that date, set another one, missed that one, and so on and so forth. The purpose of creating a timeline wasn't for me to stay married to the plan, (though ideally, that would have been lovely). The reality is that life continued to happen, things came up, I lost focus and found myself having to realign and adjust in order to move forward. Regardless of what was going on in my life, I didn't give up on my plan. I continued to work towards it and made a commitment that I would see it through to completion.

Lesson: Eliminate (or minimize) all distractions by any means necessary.

In order for you to manifest your dreams, a certain level of commitment and dedication is required. Working towards your dreams is a process. Even when distractions arise, you must remain committed to your vision, willing to do what you said you would, long after the initial feeling has subsided. It is not something that you can start today and forget about tomorrow. Every day you should be working towards the future you dream about. Rome wasn't built in a day, but there is much that can be done in one day. Every day you put off is a day wasted and a day you will never get back.

There are many things that ask for your time and attention like your children, your partner, your work, even television, cell phones, and social media, but how much time do you dedicate to your dreams? You will continue to be flooded and bombarded with distractions to interrupt the flow of your journey. Your attention has been drawn to things outside of yourself and your destiny to keep you from moving forward. It is up to you to decide what and/or who you give your attention to.

You do not have to process all information you receive. You don't like the news? Stop watching. Don't like the music? Stop listening. Don't like the food? Stop eating it. You don't like gossiping with your friends? Stop engaging. You always have a choice, another option other than the one being presented to you.

This does not mean that life shouldn't be fun or exciting. Our experience of fun changes over time as we grow and mature. The things that may have been fun for you five years ago may no longer have the same appeal. Like everything else in life, our experience of what it means to have fun changes over time.

Be committed to the path you're on. Your future isn't going to create itself. If you are not actively working towards it, you will be stuck and life will pass you by. You can manifest the future you envision by choosing to move forward. You already have everything you will need. Make a commitment today to work (or continue the work) on your future vision.

DREAM, PLAN, ACT

"When things seem the hardest you are the closest to

your success."

~First Lady Michelle Obama~

Once I decided to take a leap of faith and started the walk towards pursuing my dreams, I was met with lots of challenges, setbacks, and disappointments. I did not allow this to discourage me from remaining committed to my journey. I rested, but I did not quit. Being a dreamer required me to step outside of my comfort zone and face my fears, over and over again. This meant doing what others refused to do in order to get the job done. Even when people I'd come to rely on for support, encouragement, and motivation weren't able to uplift me, I knew I had to encourage myself.

I've always been a writer, but it took awhile for me to find my voice and believe in myself. The moment I believed I could express that voice, I did. During earlier years in my life, I recall saying, "I can't wait to be sixteen" and then as each year passed, I couldn't wait for the next desired age until one day I finally stopped wishing for the future and started living in the present.

I started working towards the goal that my childhood self dreamed of. I regained my confidence and my love for poetry and books. I was experiencing a joy and peace that I hadn't felt in years. Though I had created a detailed plan for my life, nothing happened according to the plan.

I thought I'd have my Ph.D. before 30, making a decent salary, and living out my dreams. Instead I'd dropout of a doctoral program, was married with a child, working as a freelancer writer, but I was happy.

Somehow although things veered off course, I ended up right where I needed to be and perhaps where I always wanted to be.

Not all plans I had for my life played out accordingly, but that didn't stop me from planning. Having a plan has provided guidance and direction to the future I dream about. It has helped me navigate through uncharted territory with clarity and discernment. You have to be willing to be flexible and make adjustments to your plans. I accept life as it happens, good, bad, or indifferent, and I continue to move forward, perhaps a bit bruised, but not broken and ready to face the next challenge.

Once I decided to invite God into my life, I was able to tap into the power within. I was able to improve my connection and flow of communication with God, by spending more time inwardly in stillness, waiting to hear that quiet voice. The more I listened, the louder the voice became. All I had to do was walk towards it each day. It was in solitude that I received what I needed to move forward. I didn't have to wander aimlessly down a path without any clue of where I was heading. All that was left was to take action and begin to do the work.

As a child, I used to love puzzles. I would spend a great deal of time working on putting the outer pieces together and then work towards the center, adding piece after piece, until the puzzle was complete. Comparing this method to life, we cannot neglect the outer world on our path of inner work. That's how I approached writing this book, like a puzzle. I started with the outer edges, aspects of my story that was most accessible and then gradually worked deeper inside until I was able to bring the bigger picture to focus.

Commitment is a scary thing. Once I committed to writing this book I had to see it through to completion. I had to honor my word to complete the dream of my eleven-year-old self. This has been a huge milestone and I would not have been able to see it through without planning for it and taking action. I had to work diligently on a daily basis to face my fears head-on in order to move forward, and through all the uncertainty and doubt, I prevailed.

This is my journey, but it's not for me. It is building my testimony so that I can be of service to inspire and uplift you to remain steadfast on your journey so that you will know that it is not by your own power and strength, but by God's. He is guiding you, protecting you, building you, strengthening you, keeping you, holding you, and letting you know that everything will be okay. He's doing the same thing for us all.

Lesson: Your dreams are as reliant on you as you are on them. Get to work.

The things you focus on are the things that will ultimately be created. You cannot focus on too many things at once and expect good results. If you want to learn how to juggle, you wouldn't start off trying to juggle with three balls in your hand. Instead, you would start off with two balls and then you would get the rhythm and then you would add another, then another. Focus comes with discipline. What discipline have you exercised to create your future? When we focus on too many things, it clouds our judgment and prevents us from moving forward.

The way to begin working towards your future is by putting effort into at least one or two of your goals each day. Every day you can do something directly related to the goals you want to accomplish. If you want to start a business, have you registered for a workshop about entrepreneurship? Have you talked to someone that has started a business that you can have as a potential mentor? Have you read a book related to entrepreneurship? These are all things that you can do today to work towards getting your vision off the ground.

As you continue on your journey, life will not always follow your plans so smoothly and you'll reach a point where your life will veer off course.

Relationships change, people pass on, and the life you've envisioned may feel like it's falling apart. In these moments, when things change, seemingly unexpectedly, they can be traumatic, painful, and depressing. Understand that these changes may be part of a higher plan, though not a part of your personal plan. In these moments, we move through it, trusting and knowing, that everything has a purpose. Although you may not know what that purpose is, everything in life is divinely orchestrated. The Universe was created with a divine purpose and that includes you. Your life was given to you to manifest the greatness that exists within you. You do not have to fight for it or beg for it, but you will have to work for it.

It is important to remember that not everyone will understand and support you. Be willing to give yourself the encouragement and motivation that you need to bring your dreams to fruition. Others may not see your vision, but your dreams are not for them; they are for you. Do not allow anyone to project their fears onto you. As long as you believe in yourself, take action and work towards your goals, your dreams will manifest.

There will always be times that make you question your vision and you may feel like giving up. You'll experience letdowns and setbacks, but you shouldn't let this hinder you. It takes a lot of hard work, dedication, and commitment to bring your dreams to fruition, they do not magically happen overnight. When you find yourself at a crossroad, allow yourself time for rest, relaxation, and reflection, but do not give up. You are closer than you think to the greatest vision of your life. Steadfast! Onward and upward!

EPILOGUE

In life, we are offered two paths. One path is circular, leading to stagnation, insanity, and some form of death; while the other path leads to new experiences, growth, and abundance. Many people choose the path that is a never-ending loop; as you walk on this path there is a repetitious cycle of experiences that you have to make decisions on. Though the experiences may appear to be different, they are enhanced replications of things you've yet to learn. That is to say, you experience the same things over and over again until you recognize the patterns within your choices.

At this juncture, usually due to a significant life event, you are given an opportunity to either continue making the same choices or to choose to walk the road less travelled. Recognizing that your choices haven't gotten you any further along in life, there is a sense of urgency to do something different and if the opportunity goes unseized you will fall back into the vicious cycle you are trying to escape.

Life is your classroom and you're taught lessons to educate you in areas you haven't yet mastered. As you move through life, each lesson will provide an added level of understanding and wisdom. Most people do not consider furthering their education upon completion of formal schooling. They feel they've learned all they need to know and that there's not much more to be gained. In life's school the educational experience doesn't end, there will be more to learn. You should never stop seeking to learn more and must be willing to pursue experiences that will enhance your personal development. Formal education only provides the basic tools you'll need to survive, but you don't just want to survive, you want to thrive! Thriving requires seeking answers to questions yet to be discovered and continuing to learn as you progress along your journey.

The beauty of life is that we will never have all the answers to everything. Accept that you may not have all the answers, and allow your curiosity and sense of wonder to guide your exploration into uncharted territory, discovering yourself and wonders of the world. You will find there's much to learn and more than meets the eyes.

Each piece in the puzzle of your life fits perfectly together to form a beautiful picture. Everything you've experienced and endured in life was to form this picture. You may see a piece that seemingly doesn't fit perfectly and want to give up, but nothing in your life is a mistake. When it becomes too hard to envision the overall vision, we're inclined to quit, but if we stop working before we finish the puzzle we never get to see the finished product.

You are not the architect of your life, you are the designer. The architect draws the blueprints and builds the masterpiece, the designer gives color and flavor to the interior. Ask for direction and guidance from God so together you can create the ultimate masterpiece. Consult with the architect so your vision is not flawed or delayed.

God is waiting for you to plug in and receive the blessings that have been stored away. Spend time in stillness to hear the voice of God. Close your eyes, take a deep breath, and allow the life force of God to flow through you.

Life is intended for you to enjoy it, not to get hung up on the fence refusing to move forward. Now is the time. Whether you have intentions of getting your business in order, initiating a spiritual practice, removing yourself from distractions and negativity, stepping forward with grace and conviction knowing that your best days are ahead of you, or whatever your work may be, now is the time to do away with being good enough and get started (or continue your walk) on your journey. You were not born to be *good enough*. You were born to be great. Walk in greatness.

AFTERWORD

There's not a box big enough for you to fit in. Your greatness cannot be defined. You are an unlimited flow of potential and you have the whole Universe inside of you. You have the power to create anything and everything that you want to see manifest in your reality. You are greatness and the moment you choose to walk in that, great things will start to unfold. Strive towards your greatness. It is already within you.

Read your story backward and be grateful for all the times you have gone through, the good and bad. It is a blessing that you are here in the land of the living, your spirit lives on, and you are alive! I am thankful that you are here! I praise God for you.

ABOUT THE AUTHOR

Sharon Elise's formal education began at Kean University, where she received both her bachelors and masters degrees in Psychology in 2008 and 2012, respectively. During her time at Antioch University in New Hampshire, where she enrolled to pursue a doctorate degree, Sharon deepened her spiritual and holistic practice.

Sharon has been a guest speaker for several organizations speaking on topics such as wellness, purpose, and empowerment. She co-founded a women's empowerment group, hosted Meetup groups focusing on wellness, and received formal training as a doula and yoga instructor.

Sharon's love for writing and curiosity on how the mind works has transformed throughout her career as a writer and creative leader. Sharon continues to strengthen her journey through workshops, courses, and trainings in the art of healing, finding purpose, and total body wellness. Connect with Sharon via her website at www.sharonelise.com or email at sharon@sharonelise.com.

www.ingramcontent.com/pod-product-compliance
Lightning Source LLC
Chambersburg PA
CBHW061146040426
42445CB00013B/1575